MEANDERING SILENCE

SOUL SPEAKS

MRS. RACHANA CHAKRABORTY

ISBN 979-888521681-4

This book of Poems is a compilation of thoughts and expressions from diverse genres.

I sincerely dedicate this book to my Mother, my Sister, my Daughters, and my Husband.

Contents

Contents

Foreword

A book of collective and collaborative thoughts which transports us to different horizons.

Preface

This book is a collection of poems . A few of the Poems ,Published in the book was also awarded in various 'literary contest' . I tried to open out my heart with my spoken words. Tried using very mundane words to highlight my feelings. It will not be wrong to state, 'My feelings are expressed in words.'

Disclaimer: The contents of the book are my personal view. They do not necessarily reflect the views of the others though incertain compositions you may be able to resonate with it . I am responsible for any omissions or errors made by me, Notion Press does not assume any liability or responsibility for the same.

*All the images are used from Google.

Acknowledgements

"Meandering Silence" is a compilation of poems composed by me from te year 2019 to 2021. I would like to extend my thanks to our proofreaders and editors who had helped me in this venture.

I would also like to thank our publisher Notion Press for giving us a platform to publish our work.

And I am immensely thankful to Andrew Scott for sharing his wonderful review .

Prologue

This book is a collection of poems which covers several genre as per the emotional call. You will be captivated by the pictorial glimpse and appropriate amalgamation of words which cries out the happiness, pain and sorrows of the soul. It is rather a soul connect. Mostly all the poems are in Free Verse .

1. DELIRIOUS PAST

Past..

How can we decide
what we can do
I know I need not prove
as I very well know my
potentiality.......
but why sometimes we
are deviated by our past

which wants to cling to us
without our knowledge
why can't we move ahead
why can't we forget our past??????

2. TWO LETTERED ENERGIZER

Parenting

A new look incurred to my being,
When I got to be known by my doing
I was adorned, praised, and admired,
When you dominated my being.
I know not how to thank you, my angels
As you came and I got to be known as MA….
With a new zeal for this life,
I hope Lord gives me the right strength to face the strife.

It's not easy to run this terrain,
Of being your Ma and shaping your future.
It's the only endeavor that delights me,
And happy am I to see them rise…
And thus prove myself in making a better MA….
The new post can't be changed or altered,
What matters is a new feeling.
Can I Flemish my task endowed?
Can anyone flag me for the task endowed?
So many illusions!! So many challenges!!
But every new decision poke me back,
Am I obliviated by this new designation?
Have I placed myself on the highest podium?
I know not, I think not.
But what others say jinx me faster,
It motivates me but should I react to them further,
Or should my creation be my Pathfinder!
I think it is right to confide with my inner self,
This really comes when we are together,
And she pulls me and sweetly says MA.
I can't think of anything else after that intoxicating MA,
And jump to give them what they desire
But am I pondering them, away from their goal?
They don't like to take challenges
As they have their ultimate solution, their MA.
MA can pat, MA can put,
Every single distorted thing to be shaped,

Decades have passed but still, it is MA,
Who can create magic in their child's life.
But what about the Satan who started sowing the seeds of
Desire.
Can the two lettered energizers still hold back the cute Hands….
(Remembering those moments when I first became a mother)

3. MATHS

Parenting

Its the time its the time
To do the calculation
Deduct the tensions
Add the happiness
Divide the achievements
Multiply the developments
This is what maths has given

But this my daughter has changed
And renamed it as Tensions and Confusions
Which has made her delirious
But surprised was I when
She was explaining LPP
And even guiding her friends
So finally she agreed that
She too can relish the benefits...
Of the subject Maths.!!!!

4. SUPERMOM OR THE DEVIL'S EYE?

Parenting

Mother! Mother! When can I fly?
Mother! Mother! When can I touch the sky?"
I pondered for a while and thought,
Oh! these two were my questions when I was a child. I got up
and ran to my study to make a new start,
I tried and tried but all in vain,
Until a little demon seeded my brain,

Finally, I searched and took out the saggerly looking demonic book. It was very clear that this time I wanted to be a supermom,
And epitomize my child's dream whatever may be the cost,
I turned the pages, making some silly notes,
But lo!! After hours, I was left with huge paper heaps. I now understood that why my mom told, it was not easy to be bad
As bad had to be practiced, but good we are born with.
I once again reopened the demonic book,
And drew some geometrical shapes on the floor... Started chanting some mantras from the horrific book,
And finally, after hours of chanting the lights started flickering,
The gloom started increasing along with the smoke,
And finally, some voice asked, "Tell me your wish". I didn't miss the chance as if I was waiting for it,
I quickly told my kid's wish, which was fulfilled.
But had to sacrifice my sleep for the rest of my life!!!
I decided sleep or no sleep I will fulfill my kid's wish. My kids were happy as now they could touch the sky,
And hugged me as now, I was their supermom,
But never did they know what did I sacrifice?
And finally, after months of a sleepless night, I was about to die.
I wanted to live and enjoy my life,
But now it was too late,
I realized that though it was a noble thought,
But going the wrong path was absolutely wrong.

5. POSITIVE VIBES

Parenting..

My Granny...
My granny, oh! My granny what should I say about her
She, a lady of extreme cuteness
Concealing all her sorrow behind her smile...
Oh how she super handily smiles all her woes out,
Conceived my Mother when she herself was just a teen
But never did she complain about her extending breed.

Nine kids did she not only conceive but also managed to give them a better life,
How she could manage all her nine when I get drowned sometimes by my only two!!!!!
My Mother...
Oh my my!!! My mother personifies womanhood,
A caregiver with super organizational skills
A bundle of unbridled energy and compassion
She really is the epitome of sacrifice,
Till today I failed to learn how she does it all!!
I the mother quarrel with my daughters over petty things,
But she sacrificed her teenage for her siblings
And the rest of her life on us,
Oh...can there be any woman who doesn't know what they want?
My mom supports her own mom and to date my support system…
A real woman is she, Lucky am I to be born to her
And lucky are the persons associated with her,
She demands an aura of respect around her though her physique refutes it all.
I salute her to be beside me always!!!!

MY SISTER

Here's a noble soul who caressed me,
Lighted my darkened obliterated way

Never thought about her happiness
A little naughty, a little cute but clever all the way
Modesty covers her from head to toe
Besides me always whenever I need
A holy soul, a pure heart a crazy sis,
Thanks for being beside me..........

6. PERIOD PAINS ARE BEST MUMMY AND NOW I KNOW IT.

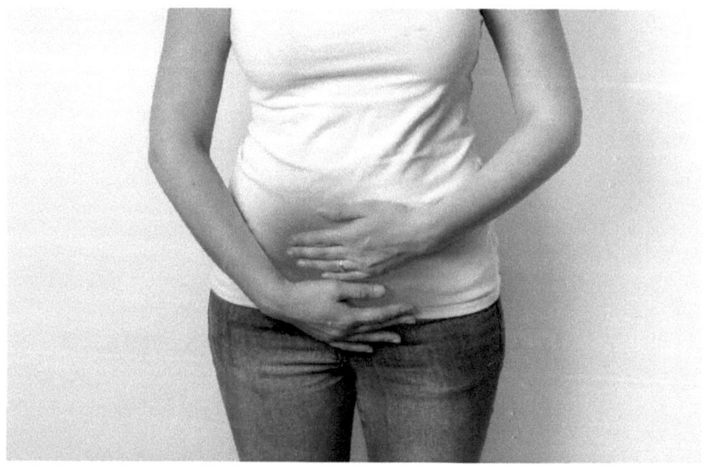

Parenting

Oh no Mama! What is this?
Why am I punished and not him?
Why am I in pain only, Why not he?
Why do I keep bleeding without any aim?
Beta, every tiny creation has a valid reason

And you can be no exceptions,
Why do you grief? Oh! My baby,
There surely is a definite reason.
But, I don't like when I bleed,
My friends keep whispering behind me
Those wretched seven days
Must never be allowed to peep.
My baby, don't be so rude
As God had specially created us,
And definitely, He had a wider vision
Hence he selected us, as we are the strongest section.
Oh! Is it really true mama?
That God loves us a little more,
And hence gave us the special powers
Making us bleed for a definite reason
Now, I believe that you understood
That we stand second to God
As it is we who can create our own progenies!
I am quite sure now that you are proud to be a girl.
Oh! Yes, Mamma, I am really proud
As now I know that I bleed for a boisterous cause,
I really don't care about my pain anymore,
As a little pain is okay for a new being.

7. THE COSMIC WAR OF HAIR CUT

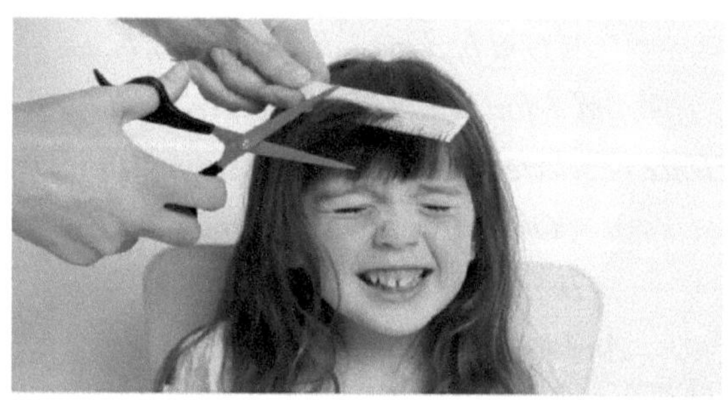

Parenting

My heart throbbed a bit louder,
And the scissors in my hand trembled,
I looked around and saw my daughter's cribbing face.
Only God knows how I overcame.
Somehow I composed myself,
And asked, is it all right beta?
She didn't answer but her eyes did,
As if telling me this is what you need...
I reverted her eyes and told her,

Beta, you are looking like a cute doll beautiful and bold.
My elder one chuckled from behind and said,
Oh! Look at the scrambled hair!!
I turned to stop her from saying so,
As this would promulgate my younger one's woe
But she, somehow irresponsible, went on giggling low
I on the other side taking an upper hand, tried to change the situation,
And very delicately asked her, How about a new style.
She again gave me a dangerous look making me stop
Any further discussions related to her dear hair,
But soon at that moment came to her Dad staring at her
And without even thinking, boldly told, your mummy really cuts well

,

But my young tigress could not take any more and shirked at him and told him Go back,
Instantly did he disappear saying, my tigress is angry
The difficult errand now seemed a bit too much,
As now, I too struggled to maintain the proper line
Teaching students seemed an easier task than this experimental scissors in hand,
Tormented I finally thought that I should stop as the decreasing length
Shattered her calm and finally did she break down pouring it all out,
My elder one though tried to console her by telling baby don't cry,

Mamma will surely make it right and sister you should not forget
That hair comes only to go, just see how mammas goes.
Finally did she smile amidst her flow, but she reminded me of my ageing baldness
But, let it go, if baldness brings my daughter's calm why not enjoy the calm.
So, finally things seemed in place and the mission too accomplished
But now when I saw my creative art, it reminded me how unsteady I was,
I couldn't help much as this indicated more of cut.
I gave up telling some other day I will do the finishing touch,
My younger one sprang up, No she said sternly
I will adjust with all your faulty cuts, but mamma please no more cut.

8. FEELINGS

Life

The old hogs are happy to be praised,
They rejuvenate and feel great.
Praise from a friend
Makes them stronger,
The day unfolds and the nature
Looks as bright as their future.
The praise from the opposite sex
Makes them pump out of their box,
Floating in the sky,

To overcome the hangover.

9. SOUL MATE

Life

I don't understand what to say,
As every moment of my life is a daiquiri.
I think and think, but where is my man?
In the long run, got hold of many roommates,
But not one to touch my soul.
People tell me I am dastardly,
In my search, as my mate

Is variegated with my dreams.
I dream but sometimes I ask
Did everybody get their soulmates???????

10. LORD OF STRENGTH

Life

When I was disturbed you guided me,
When I was lazy you gave me energy,
When I was angry you drew me away from it.

Why O lord ! now you seem to be busy
Why O Why you seem to be confused?
Why do I get your vibes only sometimes?
When I need you I always feel your presence,
Then Lord of positivity, Why can't I reach out to you?

11. RAIN

NATURE LOVE

Grains of water
Trickling down my hands
Making my heart beat a bumping
Across the merry land
Little drops of water
Pour a little better
The merry lands are thumping
The busy feet goes jumping
But why am I in bands
All over. Why should I go a little later

Rain! O Rain ! do listen to my plea
Wait a little more for me to feel
The moist trickling my hands to my face

12. SCORCHING HEAT

NATURE LOVE

The heat jumps making us abandon,
Only water can save us from the abattoir.
We plan every summer, but always there is a backlog,
We involve in badinage to forget the heat,
But the increasing heat baffles us.
We try to wear various balaclava,
But in the long run, we end
Parching our thoughts.....
Will water save us ???????
Or do we have to use technology

In limits.......

13. INTOXICATE ME

Romantic

I want the heavenly feel
I want the earthly heal
I could pay anything If only I could seal
All the negative deals.
The colorful canopy
Intoxicates the day
Coaxing me to lull my dreams
Which were once my cozy creams.
I wonder, if I could at forty plus,

Enjoy those cozy touch, traveling by bus
Or maybe a small kiss on my brow
On the great day called Valentine's day.
Growing up in traditional vibes
Never thought about public tribes
But now the love colours intoxicate me
Making me think like a wannabe.
I presume that I can't talk about love
As it is the term only for young doves.
But still am confused, that am I old for love?
My man smiles and tells, forget all this, let's go to the club.
I looked at him and he at me
As if telling me why the permutations and combinations?
Love is metaphysical so just be glee
It does nothing but teaches us to have patience.
I never experienced the dewdrops of love
But have seen my students moan in love
Oh! How so young but still allowed
Then why am I forbidden to talk about love?
My teenage days were spent at home
Though was sometimes allowed to Rome
But was strictly told, "your partner should be your tribe"
And never did I ever get excited by friendship's bribe.
The days of courtship was only through phone
As a meeting, sitting, talking, walking was always lone,
Never was I allowed to meet him, before our bond
So used to talk to his photo, and this was also my fond.

So the long dreamy days of folded love
Soon would be unfolded after the marriage curve.
Oh! but lo! My world of love was drenched,
When I discovered that my man too could never quench.
He celebrated love in the four walls of the room
And I always wanted to celebrate love with a big boom.
Two decades have crossed teaching him how to pose,
How many more to just get a tight hug and a small rose.

14. KITCHEN HEAT

Romantic

Ablaze I go with your pampering touch
The seeds of good food are about to reap
As your warm breath reconciles behind me,
I recall Nushrat's style of cutting chicken. But he alone,
And we a company.
I smell not the roasted chicken, but the sweat of your body.
Your romance puffs like the sagacious chicken in the pan
Every moment together is precious, but the heat in the kitchen is different

It brews up with the reddened chicken in flame
The rice is all cooked and finally time to let the ambiance out.

15. CREATING A MASTERPIECE

Mystery..

The dark canopy ..... Was growing darker over time
Tried to add some bright colors

But my invigorating(more energetic) thoughts crumbled it more
Splashing the colors together making it shabby
I tried to blot the splashed color but it somehow reached the other one
Oh! How I wished I had the real colors which never gets splashed
Whichever canvas you use.
I looked at my creation and tears rolled down
Pondering, my work would have had been a masterpiece
If only I had my motivation around
The darkness increased more with those thought of vagueness
Making my hands stiffer and my lips paler
I took colors more but now the darkness had invaded my mind
Stopping me from my creation
I sat down blank for a while in a pensive mood
And then for a second closed my eyes dreaming of my true love…
And lo! The darkness did go and I found myself once again in the jocund company
The canvas was enlightened like my gleaming eyes and a hidden smile
Nothing now could stop me from creating the masterpiece
My heart too danced like the newly created masterpiece
Finding my true love was bliss in my solitude.

16. WAITING FOR YOU

Romance

The minute's changes to hours,
The hour's change to days,
The day changes to months,
But still, the wait is on.
Why O why! you enjoy,
Seeing me in pain stumbling just,
To hear from you.
Your voice changes me,
And glides me to my fantasy.
But you... Oh! so selfish

Never gives me a single chance
But just keeps me waiting for you
You know me very well
I won't stop, but still, you want me to WAIT...

17. WHY CAN'T I DREAM ABOUT YOU….?

Romantic

I know not why I get lazy,
As thoughts about you always drive me crazy,
I do try to drive myself away
Penalizing me to the endless bay.
The craziness increases with the passing time,
Nevertheless, I know you will never stop paying your fine,
Though so far apart are we, why can't the eagerness prolong,

I hope that it might be a long dream, and will soon be awakened by a big gong.
Promise me those days of glee,
Awaiting for you in the endless plea,
The road to you seems obliviated, but will the quest ever end,
I am happy to be with you in dreams, but don't know why you never send..
The messages from you make me quench my thirst,
But you just seem to get disturbed always ready to burst,
Why can't you allow me to be happy with you in my dreams?
Do you think, thereto I have someone hidden in my wings??......

18. CONFUSED LOVE

Romantic

I want to express my love to you, but why don't you value,
I love your cozy arms, but does that mean I need you for sex!!
Why can't Love just be love…
Oh! why can't you just lend me your arms, which is also love
That cozy arms wooed me always,
But I really don't know. how you don't know?
You say you need time but still can't make out Why,

I need your cozy touch, I want to feel your arm,
I don't know will you ever understand my Love?
Love is calm, love is peace, love is that sweet music,
But every time I come near you, I don't know why you want sex,
If I don't reciprocate you go cross, But tell me is love all about sex?

19. YOU MAKE MY HEART LEAP

Romantic

He never says, he never shows,
He never said those three golden words.
But still, his love for me is divine.
I never can stop craving it.
He hides his love....but still I see,

He hides his feelings....but still I sense,
He hides his emotions....but still I feel,
Can he ever understand... His hiding nature pulls me to Him.
He treats me like a teenager,
He pampers me like a child.
He senses my untold agony,
What more can I expect?
But still, he never says the golden words of love,
He never poses for a close-up pic,
He never is the first one to wish for those special days,
But still, his love is what I crave.

20. LOVE UNTOLD

Romantic

He never says, he never shows,
He never said those three golden words..
But still, his love for me is divine.
I never can stop craving it.
He hides his love....but still I see,
He hides his feelings....but still I sense,
He hides his emotions....but still I feel,
Can he ever understand... His hiding nature pulls me to Him.

He treats me like a teenager,
He pampers me like a child.
He senses my untold agony,
What more can I expect?
But still, he never says the golden words of love,
He never poses for a closeup pic,
He never is the first one to wish for those special days,
But still, his love is what I crave.

21. THE BOND THAT CAN NEVER UNBIND

Romance

I and you,
You and me,
when together, what do we need?
Rules, O! the wretched rules,
Do we need it dear, in our deeds.
Rules are rigid, but I am happy to see
You smiling at me,

I am dying to be in your cozy arms,
It is the only place where I can plead
And it is the only place where you are calm.
I know, you know, we all know,
That we don't need to read
any books,
no need to demonstrate
My love for you,
for decades, it will tread
I just need to be with you,
Hold me close to your heart, a little closer
Why should we be bothered about the woes?
My rules only bend to you
I know your rules too
bend to me.
What should we care about dear, let our lips say
the glorious two decades we celebrate in a lip lock.
Do we ever need to unfold our untold story?
Of our ever nourishing love
fortifying with the growing years
I know our love will never fade
and that we will pervade all the gates
And combat to a romantic bliss even after our sweet twenties
The only rule we follow is that we care about "US," just,
I and you,
You and me
when together, what do we need?

22. BESIDES YOU...

Romance

Time doesn't seem to move, since I met you,
Your face keeps reverberating in my eyes since I met you.
Like a magnet, you draw me closer to you.
So close that I can't move my eyes from you.
I hope this fervor doesn't wilt,
I hope this distance doesn't tilt,
Our equation, endearment, and empathy...
I yearn for you, I desiderate for you.
Oh, time can you fly now,
And transport me to the arms of my love.

Summary

The book of poems is a journey to your inner self . It is the subdued feelings of the soul. The soul needs many things but it is not able to express ,so spoken words are the best resourse.

Reviews By Established Authors

Grant Wass

Grant H Wass. is a poet. He is a poet not to the world but to himself. He shares his life, and his voice through his words, and his nightmares to anyone who is brave enough to read them.

He lives in America, out west a ways. Where the air is hot, cold, and breathable.

His Review about Meandering Silence:

I didn't read this book, Instead, I took a beautiful journey through it. My feelings never stalled, for I willingly road the wind into every word alive, with so many emotions and truth. I am now free to feel.

With thoughts of love and light,

Grant H Wass

Dr.Ampat Koshy

Dr. Koshy A.V. who was working as an Assistant Professor in the English Department of Jazan University, Saudi Arabia, has 25 books with his name on the cover, 3 degrees, 1 diploma, and many certificates, prizes, awards, and nominations to his credit and also, besides teaching, is an editor, anthology maker, poet, critic, and writer of fiction. He runs an autism NPO with his wife, Anna Gabriel besides being managing editor for Fasihi. Two of his co-authored books published in 2020 were Amazon best-sellers in India and USA, namely, Wine-kissed Poems with Jagari Mukherjee and

Vodka by the Volga with Santosh Bakaya. His latest achievements are his anthologies as editor of TSL's Roseate Sonnet Anthology and Ruddy Ravens plus a certificate from Italy for best foreign language poem. He instituted the Reuel International Poetry Prize in 2014 and founded The Significant Anthology.

His Review about Meandering Silence:

Rachana Chakraborty has put together a bouquet of poems through which I got to know about her daughters, mother, grandmother, husband, and her love for art and poetry as well as "Maths". Her poetry is a fascinatingly "spontaneous outpouring of emotions" in free verse about parenting and romance and love. Many of the poems are autobiographical in miniature. From them, we get to know her mind, heart, soul, and spirit intimately. A poem on cutting her daughter's hair is humorous and the one on Maths is thought-provoking. In one poem she asks the question boldly which all women want to ask which is why the lover needs sex and cannot be satisfied with or understand love. She also asks another question in one poem that is pertinent, which is can only young girls fall in love and enjoy the experience. She also compares the past with the present and tells us how in her younger days she could only look at a photograph and how modernity has made everything different. All in all, her poems are very interesting to read, and easy to grasp and quickly read and finish, or complete, as a group; as they center around three themes, a pleasant poetic wool-gathering that brings us moments of unexpected treasure and human connection. And isn't that what poetry is all about, the language by which readers and writers connect with each other in our humanness directly, many a time?

Ms.Barnana Acharjee

An educator by Profession for the past two decades and a writer by passion, an ardent animal lover and finds reclaim in Nature's lap. She believes Nature heals.

Her Review about Meandering Silence:

A wonderful collection of neatly woven words into a finely knit cardigan of poems...

Written in free verse she has opened up her world to the readers.

Easy to read and understand, her poems are like a journey taken into her life at different stages and phases..

I wish her all the very best for her future.

Dr Nawab Md, Dilawar Hasan

Dr Nawab Md, Dilawar Hasan,

MD.(Distinction), D.I.H., has over forty-three years of Clinical and Laboratory experience both in Public and Private practice. Besides clinical papers and presentations, he has nurtured his literary zeal with two books; one, an autobiography and, the other, an anthology of poems; both in Assamese. Besides, he has translated one into English, reviewed three Medical books, and edited five souvenirs. As a freelance writer, he has contributed articles both in English and Assamese. Music and Cricket are his other interests.

His Review about Meandering Silence:

" Meandering in Silence", is a wonderful and candid reflection of the poet's inner- self. The poems composed recently (2019-2021), have principally dwelt on basic experiences of parenting, life, love, romance, nature-love, and mystery -that enriched her womanhood at various stages.

First and foremost, one finds a beautiful exposition of happiness, joy, pride, and motivation of her motherhood and delightful parenting in a few selected poems. These are replete with her motherly care, love, help, inspiration, and guidance offered to her two young daughters while growing up, both in happy and troubled times. She is equally aware of the perils of her being a 'supermom' as also, of sacrificing a great deal of her own 'space' during their upbringing. However, she was fortunate enough to have her granny and her mother for their unconditional and unflinching support in her own life. She draws inspiration from them.

Reflecting on ' life,' 'love', ' romance', ' mystery' and ' nature-lover in several other poems, she lays bare her true inner- self vividly, with all her delicate, subtle, passionate, and intense feelings. The incidents and episodes, though personal, strike the innermost chord of the universal woman. The agonizing quest for true love, the sublime feelings of the Lord overhead, the ' bliss of solitude' that lights up her gloomy mind as well as her canvas in front, are true reflections of her soul-searching endeavors. They portray the poet's ever-inquisitive and restless mind in search of a distant heavenly bliss.

On the contrary, the romance of feeling the 'touch' and 'puff' of her beloved partner alongside the rising heat of the kitchen -fire, brings out her highly sensual and sensitive emotions.

Witty and fun-loving at heart, she equally gives a delightful twist to her lost opportunities of the Valentine days of yore, by teaching her present husband about how to pose while offering her the Valentine's 'roses '.

These beautiful feelings are invariably accompanied by matching images. Her language is simple, transparent, and lucid. Her expressions are spontaneous and down-to-earth without any complex or ineligible similes or imageries and, yet, vibrant and appealing. Hope the readers will enjoy each and every poem with pure delight.

Andrew Scott

Andrew Scott

Andrew Scott is a native of Fredericton, NB. During his time as an active poet, Andrew Scott
has taken the time to speak in front of classrooms, judge poetry competitions as well as be
published worldwide in such publications as The Art of Being Human, Battered Shadows and
The Broken Ones. His books, Snake With A Flower, The Phoenix Has Risen, The Path, The
Storm Is Coming, Through My Eyes and Searching are available now

His Review about Meandering Silence:

Rachana Chakraborty has weaved together a great tapestry of words in Meadering Silence. With such themes as romance, parenting, and life, Meandering Thoughts is thought-provoking and touching.

This is a work that is very enjoyable and recommended for everyone.

Dianna Bellerose

Dianna Bellerose

Dianna Bellerose was born and raised in eastern Europe to a working-class family. She spent most of her childhood with her grandparents.

In 2004, she graduated from Edmonds Community College with an Associates of Arts degree. She is fluent in three languages and enjoys gardening, photography, drawing, and exploring other cultures. She has a passion for writing about families and the obstacles they face in their lives, which has led her to also coach individuals in achieving their own dreams and finding their purpose.

Dianna is a well-known author of "Fire and Ice", which was an award winner NABE in the winter of 2012. She has been featured on Women's Essence Magazine in the August issue of 2012 and in Angie's Diary Online Magazine in the July 2013 issue for her achievements with this book.

She was awarded an award on March 16, 2019, for being one of the 100 most Successful Women on a Global level.

In April 2019, she was featured in the first magazine in India for being one of the ten most influential women leaders in the world

--

Blogtalkradio:http://www.blogtalkradio.com/diannabellerose

Website:http://www.diannabellerose.com

Blogger:http://www.authordiannabellerose.blogspot.com

FB:http://www.facebook.com/diannabellerose

Twitter:http://www.twitter.com/diannabellerose

Linkedin:http://www.linkedin.com/pub/dianna-bellerose/45/92/632/

Books

Contact:http://www.vcita.com/v/fd87fabf6e86a2c5/online_scheduling?staff_id=c4f7504fa081dfd3

"The best way to find yourself is to lose yourself in service of others"-Mahatma Gandhi

Her Review about Meandering Silence:

Rachna Chakraborty is a very talented author and her mastery of crafting a beautiful, meaningful poem is very unique. Rachna's poems are family-oriented and the idea is to educate by highlighting the most important things a parent should know about.

Printed by Libri Plureos GmbH in Hamburg,
Germany

9 798885 216814